THE POOH GET-WELL BOOK

THE POOH
GET-WELL BOOK

Recipes and Activities to Help You
Recover from Wheezles and Sneezles

inspired by the four Pooh books

by A. A. MILNE

VIRGINIA H. ELLISON

illustrations by Ernest H. Shepard

E. P. DUTTON & CO., INC.   NEW YORK

Grateful acknowledgment is made to David McKay Co., Inc. for permission to include the recipe for Thyme Syrup from *Stalking the Healthful Herbs* © 1966 by Euell Gibbons.

LIBRARY OF CONGRESS CATALOGING IN PUBLICATION DATA

Ellison, Virginia H.   The Pooh get-well book.

SUMMARY: Includes puzzles and word-fun, recipes for food and drink, and quiet activities for children sick or well. "Inspired by the four Pooh books by A. A. Milne."

1. Sick children—Recreation—Juvenile literature.   2. Cookery (Honey) —Juvenile literature.   3. Bird watching—Juvenile literature. 1. Games.   2. Cookery.   3. Bird watching.   I. Shepard, Ernest Howard, 1879–   illus.   II. Title.
RJ61.E537   649.8   73-80203   ISBN 0-525-37440-x

Published simultaneously in Canada by McClelland and Stewart, Ltd. Printed in the U.S.A.   First Edition

To Christopher David

Christopher Robin
Had wheezles
And sneezles,
They bundled him
Into
His bed.
They gave him what goes
With a cold in the nose,
And some more for a cold
In the head.
They wondered
If wheezles
Could turn
Into measles,
If sneezles
Would turn
Into mumps;
They examined his chest
For a rash,
And the rest
Of his body for swellings and lumps.

They sent for some doctors
In sneezles
And wheezles
To tell them what ought
To be done.
All sorts and conditions
Of famous physicians
Came hurrying round
At a run.
They all made a note
Of the state of his throat,
They asked if he suffered from thirst;
They asked if the sneezles
Came *after* the wheezles,
Or if the first sneezle
Came first.
They said, "If you teazle
A sneezle
Or wheezle,
A measle
May easily grow.

But humour or pleazle
The wheezle
Or sneezle,
The measle
Will certainly go."
They expounded the reazles
For sneezles
And wheezles,
The manner of measles
When new.
They said, "If he freezles
In draughts and in breezles,
Then PHTHEEZLES
May even ensue."

Christopher Robin
Got up in the morning,
The sneezles had vanished away.
And the look in his eye
Seemed to say to the sky,
"Now, how to amuse them today?"
Now We Are Six

Acknowledgments

I want to thank many, many children but especially those who helped me figure out, often unknowingly, what things help ease the hours spent in bed with a bout of sneezles, wheezles, or phtheezles. I appreciate the suggestions of those who played the games or made the things in the book—or ate or drank them. These children seem all to have one quality in common—a zest for life and living, an excitement about trying everything and about learning. I hope that spirit has infected this book.

Those children are: Vivian and Nick, Jan, Dave, and Christopher, Sarah, Ninky, and Chard Chypre, Mark and Matthew Meyer, Heather, Doug, and Rusty Law, Heidi Falk, Brian Liotard, Nicholas Ramond, Jud and Charles Parker Reis, Maureen and Parker Reis, Lisa and Lynda Buckley, Peter King, Fay DuBissette, Nell Eland, Philly and Kristin Belliard, and Jerôme Haslaye.

I want also to thank Eve Roettger, who shared her many talents with me. Her warmth, her insight, and her intelligence in making this book possible deserve more credit than I can give her here. So, too, do the Schaefers—Lisette and Nick, Hon and Lee—Beryl Barrow, Cornelia Zagat, Janet Van Duyn, Evelyn Liotard, Helen Mather, Akeita Somersille, Marguerite Hatfield, Gloria DuBissette, Jeanne Vance Davis, Marjorie Henderson, Lillian Phillips, Jane Smithers, Lee Shult, and Billie Weil.

I'm grateful for the books of Euell Gibbons and many

writers of bird books and bird guides. I am much in their debt and the debt of friends and companions who know more than I ever shall about birds and plants and everything else: Mary Wagenseller, Louise Raymond, Louise and Paul Liebold, and Dr. Margaret Jones.

Contents

III. PLEAZLES: TO MAKE AND PLAY WHILE GETTING WELL

Introduction

This book is for when you have a Sneezle, Wheezle, Phtheezle, or just a plain cold in the head, and you've run out of
things to think about. Or to do. For instance, you might,
like Christopher Robin, just have been to Africa and back
this morning, and are about to get off the boat. You feel
thirsty, even a little hungry. And you wonder what it's like
outside.

The Pooh Get-Well Book will do something about all of
that, except to tell you what it's like outside. If you begin
at the beginning of the book, you will find several Teazles,
which are riddles to guess, word games to play, and even
how to make rhyming words into short poems, such as,

> It doesn't take skill
> To swallow a pill.

On the other hand, if you're very thirsty or hungry, you
might first want to look over the menu of Strengthening
Things to Drink and Eat and choose one or two. Whether
they will strengthen you as Kanga's strengthening med-
icines did Roo and Tigger, it's impossible to tell. But
they're sure to make you feel better, and they're guaranteed
to be good at any hour of the day or night.

After eating and drinking your way through the middle
of the book, you will come to the section which ought to
outlast a sneezle, wheezle, phtheezle, or any combination
of the three. It gives you a tip on which raindrop to choose
in a Raindrop Race, how to do a little Bird-watching from

Bed, how to make your own Pooh Picture Puzzle, and a lot more.

The lot more we will let you discover for yourself. And by that time you ought to be well enough to get up. You might even like to lend the book to a friend who has a sneezle. But you need lend it *only* if your friend promises to return it, so that you have it handy, just in case.

Virginia H. Ellison

Stamford, Connecticut
March 30, 1973

I

TEAZLES:
PUZZLES, POEMS, AND
OTHER FUN WITH WORDS

They said, "If you teazle
A sneezle
Or wheezle,
A measle
May easily grow."
Now We Are Six

RIDDLES

1. How are a hill and a pill different?
2. What's the difference between a greedy Bear eating honey and a hungry Bear?
3. Why is a nail in a tree in the Hundred Acre Wood like a sick person?
4. Why is a lollipop like a good race horse?
5. Pooh, Piglet, Eeyore, Rabbit, Tigger, Owl, Kanga, Roo, and Christopher Robin were walking under one large umbrella. Why didn't they get wet?
6. Why was it that when Eeyore lost his tail, Pooh found it in the last place he looked?
7. What do Rabbits have that no other animal in the world has?
8. Which burns longer, Pooh's wax candle or his tallow candle?
9. If two's company and three's a crowd, what are four and five?

Answers to Riddles are upside down on the following page.

9. Nine.
8. Neither burns longer because both burn shorter.
7. Baby Rabbits.
6. Because he stopped looking when he found it.
5. Because it wasn't raining.
4. The faster you lick it, the faster it goes.
3. Because it's in firm (infirm).
2. The greedy Bear eats it too long and the hungry Bear longs to eat it.
1. The hill's hard to get up and the pill's hard to get down.

"Rabbit's clever," said Pooh thoughtfully.
"Yes," said Piglet, "Rabbit's clever."
"And he has Brain."
"Yes," said Piglet, "Rabbit has Brain."
There was a long silence.
"I suppose," said Pooh, "that that's
why he never understands anything."

The House at Pooh Corner

REBUS TEAZLES

1. A letter reached the post office addressed this way:

> Wood
>
> John
>
> Mass

It was delivered to the right person in the right town. What was his name and where did he live? This answer, and the answers to the other Rebus Teazles, are on the following page.

2. What word does this spell?

> B
>
> E

3. ⊔ C T ⊔

4. Read this out loud:

$$\frac{\text{Stand}}{\text{U}} \qquad \frac{\text{Age}}{\text{UR}}$$

5. Read aloud what Pooh said to a honey jar:

> O I C U R M T

1. John Underwood
   Andover
   Mass.
2. B on E
3. C on T in Ue
4. You understand, you are under age.
5. Oh, I see you are em (p) ty.

If I were John and John were Me,
Then he'd be six and I'd be three.
If John were Me and I were John,
I shouldn't have these trousers on.

—*Now We Are Six*

LITTLE WORDS FROM BIG WORDS

See how many words you can make using only the letters in any one of these Pooh names—Sanders, Piglet, Eeyore, Tigger, Rabbit, and Christopher.

Lists of examples are upside down below and on the next page. But don't look at them until you've finished your own lists.

RABBIT: bit, bar, bat, rat, brat, rib, art, bib, tar

TIGGER: get, tie, ire, rig, girt, tire, grit, it, gig

PIGLET: pig, pit, tip, lip, tie, let, get, gel, leg, peg, pet, pelt, pile, tile, gilt

SANDERS: an, and, are, ran, red, den, res, read, ear, sea, sand, send, end, rend, dean, earn, sane, dear, near, dress, darn, dare

"Do you know what this is?"
"No," said Piglet.
"It's an A," said Eeyore.
"Oh," said Piglet.

The House at Pooh Corner

C: cop, cope, cot, crop, chop, chip, chirp, corer, chore, choir, chest, core, crier, cite, chose, cost

H: her, his, hot, hoe, hip, hop, hit, hire, host, hose, hope, hoist

R: roe, rip, rot, rest, rich, ripe, rose, rope, rote, rise, resort, report, ripest

I: is, it, ire, itch

S: sit, sir, sip, sot, sop, set, stop, shot, shop, ship, spot, sire, step, stir, store, sport, sore, sort, site, sprite

T: to, top, toe, tie, tip, trip, tire, tore, this, their, torch

O: or, ore, other, ocher, optic, ostrich, octopi

P: pit, pet, pro, pot, pie, pier, post, port, pest, pose, poet, pore, pert, perch, pitch, poster, pitcher

H: (see above)

E: etch, err, escort, ethic, epic

R: (see above)

You might want to choose other long words, such as:
HEFFALUMP, BIRTHDAY, EXPOTITION, SURROUNDED,
BREAKFAST, BRACKEN, UNBOUNCED, WOLERY, ENCHANTED,
CHRISTMAS, SNEEZLES, MEASLES, BUCKINGHAM, BUTTERCUP,
DISOBEDIENCE, POLITENESS, ENGINEER, EMPEROR.

"Clever!" said Eeyore scornfully,
putting a foot heavily on his three sticks.
"Education!" said Eeyore bitterly,
jumping on his six sticks.
"What *is* Learning?" asked Eeyore as he
kicked his twelve sticks into the air.
"A thing *Rabbit* knows! Ha!"

The House at Pooh Corner

RHYMING WORDS

A good game is to think of pairs of words that rhyme and then make them into a little poem. Here is one of Pooh's Hums that uses these rhyming words: *bigger* and *Tigger; fatter* and *matter; stronger* and *longer; smaller* and *taller; habit* and *Rabbit.*

If Rabbit
Was bigger
And fatter
And stronger,
Or bigger
Than Tigger,
If Tigger was smaller,
Then Tigger's bad habit
Of bouncing at Rabbit
Would matter
No longer,
If Rabbit
Was taller.

Pooh said nothing, because he was thinking of a poem.
The House at Pooh Corner

Or, if you said the rhyming words, *things* and *wings*, you
might get a Pooh poem of your own, such as:

> Bees are *things*
> That always have *wings*.

If you had the rhyming words, *call* and *Small*, you might
write:

> I would *call*
> A beetle *Small*.

TWO-LINE POEMS

Writing two-line poems gets easier and easier the more you do it. And the more you do it, the more pairs of rhyming words you'll be able to think of.

As you read through *Winnie-the-Pooh* and *The House at Pooh Corner,* or they're read to you, you'll get ideas. Here are some samples:

> As early as sevenish
> Pooh felt elevenish.

> Whatever Pooh ate
> Made him gain weight.

> It doesn't take skill
> To swallow a pill.

"Poetry and Hums aren't things which you get, they're things which get *you*. And all you can do is to go where they can find you."

The House at Pooh Corner

Said Kanga to Roo
Are you Piglet or who?

Did Eeyore complain
About ice, snow, or rain?

The south end of Pooh
Couldn't get through.

Bees, beware!
There's a Pooh in the air.

"You'll like this piece of poetry," said Rabbit.
"You'll love it," said Piglet.

Winnie-the-Pooh

You might like to try adding the last line to each of these limericks about Pooh, Piglet, WOL, Kanga and Roo, and then making up your own. You will find the last lines to these limericks upside down.

POOH

Edward Bear is a Winnie-the-Pooh.
Under Sanders he lives like a who?
    Like a modest old Bear
    Whose favorite fare

. . . .

Is a jar of fresh honey or two.

PIGLET

The Piglet, the best friend of Pooh,
Was timider even than you
When he heard the loud thump
Of a trapped Heffalump

.   .   .   .

Whom he knew he could never subdue.

WOL

A WOL whooo was really old Owl
Told stories so long Pooh would growl
And without counting sheep
He'd nod off to sleep

.   .   .   .

Though the wind blew a blust'rous wild howl.

"For Pooh?" said Eeyore.
"Of course it is. The best bear
in all the world."

Winnie-the-Pooh

KANGA AND ROO

Roo's mother was long-leaping Kanga
Whose spring was as high as her spranga.
With Roo in her pouch
As snug as a couch

. . . .

She'd land on her tail with a banga.

"Well, you just have to talk very hard
to Kanga so as she doesn't notice anything."
"Oh! What about?"
"Anything you like."
"You mean like telling her a little bit
of poetry or something?"
"That's it," said Rabbit. "Splendid."

Winnie-the-Pooh

LIMERICKS

Now you may want to try making up limericks of your own. The trick to writing them is to rhyme the first two lines with the last or fifth line. The third and fourth lines also rhyme.

Here are two:

1.

A boy with a very sore throat
Said he'd drink only milk from a goat.
    If asked why not cow's,
    Which the doctor allows?
He'd jump in his bathtub and float.

"And that's the whole poem," Pooh said.
"Do you like it, Piglet?"

The House at Pooh Corner

2.

A girl from her pillow in bed
Called to her mother and said,
 "I feel like a whale
 Being dipped in a pail.
Is there some way to lighten my head?"

Now you try.

"Well," said Pooh, "in poetry—
in a piece of poetry—well, you *did* it,
Piglet, because the poetry says you did.
And that's how people know."

The House at Pooh Corner

II
STRENGTHENING THINGS
TO DRINK AND EAT

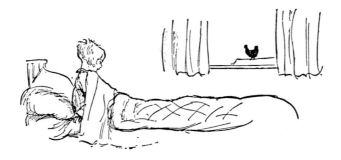

They gave him what goes
With a cold in the nose,
And some more for a cold
In the head.

Now We Are Six

THYME FOR TEA

1 teaspoon dried thyme *or*   1 cup boiling water
  1 sprig fresh   1 teaspoon honey

Put the thyme in a cup.
Add the boiling water. Let steep for 5 minutes or more on
  an asbestos pad over low heat.
Stir in the honey until dissolved.
Drink to ease a cough or a sore throat.

The tips of Piglet's ears glowed
suddenly, and he tried to say something;
but even after he had husked once or
twice, nothing came out.

        The House at Pooh Corner

TODDY FOR A COUGH

1 teaspoon honey	lemon peel
1 Tablespoon lemon juice	powdered *or* ground nutmeg,
very hot weak tea *or* water	cinnamon, *or* cloves

In an 8-ounce mug, stir the honey and lemon juice together
with a long-handled metal spoon.

Leave the spoon in the mug and pour in the very hot tea or
water.

Float the lemon peel on it.

Dust the top with a sprinkle of nutmeg, cinnamon, or
cloves.

"I didn't bounce, I coughed," said
Tigger crossly.

"Bouncy or coffy, it's all the same
at the bottom of the river."

The House at Pooh Corner

HONEY-THYME COUGH SYRUP

¼ cup dried thyme   ¼ cup boiling water
¼ cup honey

Put the thyme and the honey in a small pitcher with a long-
handled metal spoon.
Leave the spoon in the pitcher and pour in the boiling
water.
Stir and allow it to infuse until cool.
Strain into a screw-top jar and keep refrigerated.
Take a tablespoonful or two several times a day.
This is an excellent remedy for coughs and sore throats.
Sweetened thyme is the basic ingredient in many com-
mercial cough syrups. It's also one of the best.

And then quite suddenly (just like Us)
One got Better and the other got Wuss.
Good Bear muddled his Twice Times Three—
But Bad Bear coughed *in his hand-ker-chee!*
Now We Are Six

Strengthening Things to Drink and Eat   23

HONEY AND LEMON JUICE
FOR A SQUEAKY VOICE

4 Tablespoons honey   juice of 1 lemon

Stir the lemon juice into the honey until liquid.
Take a teaspoonful or more after each dose of medicine.

"Pooh!" squeaked the voice.
The House at Pooh Corner

BISCUIT-COUGH SYRUP

1 cup unsweetened fruit juice   squeeze of lemon juice
  honey

Mix the fruit juice and lemon juice.
Add the honey to taste, depending on the natural sweetness
  of the juice.
Heat but do not boil the juice and honey together until the
  honey dissolves as you stir.
Drink after taking your medicine.
On a hot day, pour the Biscuit-Cough Syrup over some ice
  cubes in a small glass.

"It was a Biscuit Cough,"
said Roo, "not one you tell about."
The House at Pooh Corner

COUGH NECTARS

FRUIT NECTAR

1 cup grapefruit juice
1 cup pineapple juice
1 cup apple juice

2 Tablespoons honey
1 Tablespoon orange
   marmalade

Combine juices, honey, and marmalade in a blender or stir
   together until thoroughly mixed.
Strain and drink.

Binker's always talking,
   'cos I'm teaching him to speak:
He sometimes likes to do it
   in a funny sort of squeak,
And he sometimes likes to do it
   in a hoodling sort of roar . . .
And I have to do it for him
   'cos his throat is rather sore.
Now We Are Six

BANANA NECTAR

¼ banana   1 cup orange juice
1 Tablespoon (or more) honey   ½ cup pineapple juice

Put the banana and honey in a blender or mash together
   until liquid. Then heat but do not boil.
Stir in the orange and pineapple juice and heat.
Drink warm or cool.

"You bounced me," said Eeyore gruffly.
"I didn't really. I had a cough,
and I happened to be behind Eeyore,
and I said, 'Grrrr-oppp-ptschschschz.' "
The House at Pooh Corner

MALTED MILK

3 Tablespoons powdered malted milk	1 glass milk

Add the malted milk powder to the milk.
Heat without boiling and take before going to sleep. Or
  may be drunk cold at other times.

And sometimes, when Kanga thought Tigger
wanted strengthening, he had a spoonful
or two of Roo's breakfast after meals as medicine.

The House at Pooh Corner

HONEY-PEACH EXTRACT OF MALT

1½ Tablespoons instant malt
   or malted milk, natural
¼ cup canned *or* fresh peach
   juice

½ teaspoon honey
1 cup milk

Mix the malt, peach juice, and honey together.
Add the milk and stir. Drink.
Delicious, cold or hot.

Which explains why he always lived
at Kanga's house afterwards, and
had Extract of Malt for breakfast,
dinner, and tea.

The House at Pooh Corner

ORANGE JUICE PHOSPHATE

1 egg	juice of 1 orange
1 Tablespoon honey	milk

Beat the egg and add the honey when the egg begins to
  froth.
Add the orange juice and beat again to mix.
Pour into a tall glass with or without ice.
Fill with cold milk.

"Now," said Kanga, "there's
your medicine, and then bed."
Winnie-the-Pooh

EGGNOGS

PLAIN EGGNOG

1 egg   milk
1 teaspoon honey   nutmeg
3 drops vanilla

Beat egg until frothy and thoroughly blended.
Add the vanilla to the honey while warming and spoon a
    small amount of the honey-vanilla into the beaten egg
    first before adding all of it.
Pour into a glass.
Add the milk, stir well, and top with a grind or two of nut-
    meg.

FRUIT JUICE EGGNOG

Instead of honey, use a teaspoon or more of sweetened rasp-
    berry, strawberry, apricot, orange, or pineapple juice
    before adding the milk to the plain eggnog. Raspberry,
    strawberry, or apricot jam is very good to use too.

COCOA EGGNOG

1 egg white, beaten stiff   1 Tablespoon honey
1 egg yolk, beaten   milk
1 teaspoon cocoa, unsweetened

Mix the cocoa, honey, and egg yolk.
Fold the egg white into the cocoa-honey blend.
Slowly add the milk, stirring all the time.

And it was eleven o'clock.
Which was Time-for-a-little-something.

The House at Pooh Corner

THE KING'S BREAKFAST

1 Royal slice of bread   marmalade *or* honey
1 pat sweet butter

A Royal slice of bread means one slice of your favorite
  bread.
Spread it with butter and eat.
A second slice could be spread with marmalade—or better
  yet, honey, especially if your throat is sore.

The King asked
The Queen, and
The Queen asked
The Dairymaid:
"Could we have some butter for
The Royal slice of bread?"
    When We Were Very Young

HONEYCOMB CHEWING GUM

1 2-inch square of honeycomb
1 Tablespoon water
2 drops oil of cinnamon,
　　clove, *or* peppermint, *or*

¼ teaspoon ground cinnamon,
　　clove, nutmeg, ginger, *or*
　　allspice
¼ teaspoon each, grated lemon
　　or orange rind and juice

Melt the wax and honey from the honeycomb in the water
　　in an enamel or non-stick saucepan. The wax will stick to
　　a metal pan.
Add the drops of spice oil or the ground spices and the
　　lemon or orange rind and juice.
Pour into a clean jar with a screw-top. When cool, spoon
　　out and chew a little of the chewing gum.
Chew until all the flavor is gone. Don't swallow.

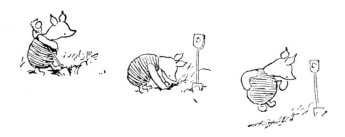

"Well," said Pooh, "if I plant a
honeycomb outside my house, then
it will grow up into a beehive."

Piglet wasn't quite sure about
this.

The House at Pooh Corner

CHICKEN AND EGG SOUP

1½ cups canned chicken soup
1½ Tablespoons each, finely chopped scallion *or* onion, celery, carrot

1 teaspoon parsley
1 egg
1 teaspoon cold water
salt, if necessary

Simmer the chicken soup or broth with scallion or onion, celery, carrot, and parsley.

Beat the egg with the cold water until yolk and white are thoroughly blended.

Add 3 Tablespoons of the hot soup to the beaten egg, one at a time. Add the rest of the soup.

Serve topped with a floweret of parsley.

This is digestible, delicious, and filling, especially with a piece of toast or a cracker.

"And how are you?" said Winnie-the-Pooh.
Eeyore shook his head from side to side.
"Not very how," he said. "I don't seem to have felt at all how for a long time."

Winnie-the-Pooh

HOT CLOVE ORANGES

(Preheat oven to 350° F.)

medium-size juice oranges   honey
6–8 cloves for each orange

Stick the cloves into the oranges.
Put them in a baking pan. Roast for about 45 minutes to 1 hour. (This can be done along with baking potatoes.)
The oranges will swell and the skin will brown, especially at the spots where the skin breaks and a little of the juice runs out.
Remove from the oven and let them cool until they can be touched comfortably.
Put an orange in a bowl. Pull it apart. Spoon honey over the warm, sweet, juicy pulp and eat.
Also good at room temperature.

YOGURT AND FRUIT

½ cup plain yogurt
  honey

½ cup puréed fresh fruit *or*
    jar strained "infant" fruit,
    such as peaches, apricots,
    applesauce, pears, prunes

Mix the yogurt and the puréed fruit in a bowl together.
Depending on how sweet you like your yogurt, add honey.

The Doctor said,
  "Tut! It's another attack!"
And ordered him Milk
  and Massage-of-the-back,
And Freedom-from-worry
  and Drives-in-a-car,
And murmured,
  "How sweet your chrysanthemums are!"
      When We Were Very Young

ISSUE-A-REWARD
LEMON-HONEY JELLIES

1 Tablespoon gelatin	1 lemon, grated rind and
¼ cup cold water	juice
⅔ cup boiling water	⅛ teaspoon salt
¼ cup honey	

Dissolve gelatin in the cold water and pour into a small
shallow pan.

Add the boiling water, honey, rind and juice of the lemon,
and salt. Stir after adding each ingredient until well
blended.

Chill overnight.

Cut into cubes for eating.

"First, Issue a Reward. Then—"

"Just a moment," said Pooh, holding up
his paw. "*What* do we do to this—what
you were saying? You sneezed just as you
were going to tell me."

Winnie-the-Pooh

AS A DESSERT

Use 1 cup instead of ⅔ cup boiling water to make the jelly.

Pour the lemon-honey jelly into small custard cups or molds.

If in season, press a small leaf of fresh mint, rose geranium, or violet onto the top of the jelly.

What is the matter with Mary Jane?
I've promised her sweets and
    a ride in the train,
And I've begged her to stop for a bit
    and explain—
What *is* the matter with Mary Jane?
When We Were Very Young

CRUSTIMONEY PROSEEDCAKE

(Preheat oven to 325° F.,
square or loaf pans)

(Preheat oven to 350° F.,
layer-cake pans)

1½ cups honey
1¼ cups cooking oil, scant
2 cups whole wheat flour
2 teaspoons baking powder
1 teaspoon baking soda
1 teaspoon salt, if nuts
unsalted
2 teaspoons cinnamon

4 eggs
3 cups scant, or 3 "junior"
jars (7½ oz.) , grated
carrots, drained
1 cup chopped nuts—pecans,
almonds, walnuts
1 cup shredded coconut
(optional)

Butter one square pan, two loaf pans, or two 9-inch cake
pans.

Mix the honey with the oil.

Sift the flour, baking powder, baking soda, salt, and cinnamon together.

Add the dry ingredients to the honey and oil mixture alter-
nately with the eggs, beating as you add them.

Beat in the carrots, nuts, and coconut.

Bake the square cakes at 325° F. for 1 hour and 10 minutes;
the loaf cakes for 1 hour or until a cake tester comes out
moist but clean; the layers at 350° F. for 20 to 25 minutes.

"What does Crustimoney Proseedcake
mean?" said Pooh. "For I am a Bear of Very
Little Brain, and long words Bother me."
—*Winnie-the-Pooh*

BANANAS WITH THISTLES
IN HONEY AND CREAM

¼ cup shredded coconut
red and blue vegetable
coloring
2 bananas
1 Tablespoon brown sugar

½ cup unsweetened pineapple
juice, orange juice,
or coconut milk
1 Tablespoon honey
cream

Put the coconut in a screw-top jar. Mix a few drops of blue
and red vegetable coloring to get a lavender or purple
tint. Pour it on the coconut. Put the screw-top on the jar
and shake until the coloring is evenly spread.

Peel and cut the bananas in half the long way and then in
quarters, and place into the juice or coconut milk in a
a heavy-bottomed skillet, non-stick frying pan, or chafing
dish.

Sprinkle with sugar and honey.

Simmer until the bananas are soft, about 4 or 5 minutes.

Serve in bowls with cream and thistle coconut.

HONEY MILK TOAST

1 cup milk	butter
1 slice bread	honey

Heat the milk but do not boil it. While the milk is heating, toast the bread and butter it.

Pour the hot milk into a warm bowl.

Float the buttered toast in the hot milk and drizzle honey over it.

Eat with a spoon.

The first thing Pooh did was to go to the cupboard to see if he had quite a small jar of honey left.

Winnie-the-Pooh

III

PLEAZLES:
TO MAKE AND PLAY
WHILE GETTING WELL

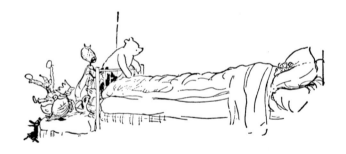

"But humour or pleazle
The wheezle
Or sneezle,
The measle
Will certainly go."

Now We Are Six

RAINDROP RACE

You can play this on a rainy day alone or when somebody's with you.

Choose a raindrop on the windowpane. Choose the one you think will get to the bottom of the pane first. If I were you, I'd choose the fattest drop, even though the fattest doesn't *always* win.

These are my two drops of rain
Waiting on the window-pane.

I am waiting here to see
Which the winning one will be.
Now We Are Six

Even when you don't feel up to doing much of anything, you may be able to see birds from your window and watch them fly or light on your window sill.

To make bird-watching fun, a bird feeder of some kind is necessary. A box with a rim an inch or so high will do on the ledge of your window. Plastic or wood are better than cardboard, even where the window ledge is protected by the overhang of the roof.

The birds won't come immediately after bird food is put out for them, but come they will, sometimes within a few hours.

If you don't have a bird book at home, perhaps someone in your family will borrow one for you from the library. Ask for a guide to the birds in your section of the country or in the United States. Be sure it has pictures in color.

Look up the birds you know—pictures and descriptions. In most bird-guides, you'll find pictures of other birds in the same family on the same page. Pick out their differences. The descriptions will give you clues you may not notice at first in the pictures.

It's a good idea to keep a notebook and crayons handy. Birds don't stand still for long. Quickly draw a picture of a bird you see, showing where its colors and markings are. Then you can look it up later in your guide. Write the name of the bird under its picture and any distinguishing points about it.

It may be that you'll enjoy this so much you'll want to continue your notebook after you're up again and able to bird-watch outdoors.

To make it easier to look up birds you don't know, here are some—

THINGS TO NOTICE

1. *Colors and Markings:* Look first at where the colors of a bird's feathers are—breast, back, rump, tail, wings, crown, cheek, throat. Does it have wing bars, streaks, or spots on its breast? Notice, too, the color of its bill, legs, eyes, and top-knot, if it has one.

2. *Size:* Is the bird smaller or larger than a bird you know? A sparrow, a robin, a pigeon, and a crow are four good sizes to use as measure.

3. *Bills:* Seed-eating birds, such as sparrows and finches, have short thick bills, often with an angle at the base of the bill for cracking seeds. Insect-eating birds, such as warblers, have thin small bills for catching insects and larger mouths than seed-eaters.

seed eater's bill

insect eater's bill

Robins, as you know, are expert at digging earthworms with their thin beaks which are also good for spearing grubs and for eating small fruits and berries. Swallows, swifts, and martins have very big mouths. As they fly, they catch the insects they live on.

4. *Tails:* Tails are of different lengths and often have distinctive markings. Some tails are pointed. Others are rounded, forked, or squared off at the end. Some stick up; others stand straight out or straight down from the bird's body.

5. *Feet and Claws* are suited to the places where a bird lives and to getting its food.

Ducks and other swimming birds have webs between their toes, so that their feet can act like paddles and let them feed in different parts of ponds or other shallow waters.

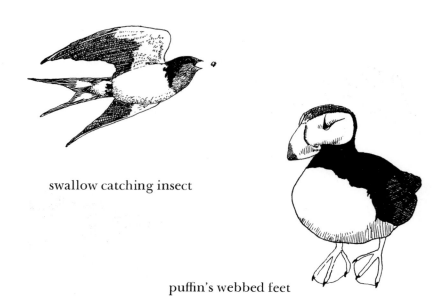

swallow catching insect

puffin's webbed feet

quail—a walking bird

sparrow—a perching bird

Walking birds, such as chickens, turkeys, and pheasants, are those that walk, run, and scratch for seeds, bugs, and pebbles. They have short nails, three long toes in front, and a "spur" or short toe higher up on the back of the leg.

Perching birds—the sparrows, finches, warblers, thrushes, chickadees, tanagers, flycatchers, blackbirds, wrens, and others—hop around in trees and on grass, and also walk, to get their food. They have four toes, three in front and one in back, with long nails which are good for holding onto a branch or twig.

Woodpeckers, which walk up and down the trunks of trees, have two toes in front and two behind, so that they can get a good grip on the bark of a tree. They move jerkily, get better grip and balance on the tree trunk by pressing the ends of their longest tail feathers against the tree.

Hawks, owls, and eagles, which catch rats, mice, frogs, snakes, reptiles, and birds with their feet and claws, have powerful, thick toes with very long sharp-hooked nails. These are good for carrying what they catch back to their nests.

woodpecker on tree trunk

hawk's sharp-hooked nails

6. *Legs:* Legs are of different colors and different lengths. The length is often suited to the place where a bird lives. Shore and wading birds, like sandpipers, yellowlegs, and herons, have longer legs than swimming birds. Walking birds have longer legs than perching birds.

You will also soon learn from watching that each kind of bird has its own pattern of flight and its own silhouette. And later on, you'll come to know their songs. There are records of these to help you pick out the different songs from the chorus of songs you hear in spring and early summer.

The birds you see from your window will depend on where you live. In spring and fall, when many birds migrate, you may see more kinds than usual. Here's a list of some common birds likely to be seen in different places.

CITIES

Pigeons, starlings, English and house sparrows, gulls (if you live near the sea or a big body of water) .

CITY PARKS AND SUBURBS

Robins, chipping and song sparrows, house wrens, yellow warblers, common grackles, purple finches. Where there are trees good for nesting: orioles, vireos, cardinals, mockingbirds. In colder climates in winter: chickadees, titmice, juncos, hairy and downy woodpeckers, sparrows, finches, cardinals, jays, mourning doves.

FARMS AND OPEN COUNTRY

In addition to those seen in parks and suburbs—flycatchers, waxwings, screech owls, bluebirds, catbirds, towhees, thrashers, grosbeaks, among many others. Near barns and sheds: barn owls, barn swallows, cowbirds. In fields and meadows: grasshopper sparrows, meadowlarks, and bobolinks. In late summer and fall: crows, hawks, blackbirds, snow buntings.

EVERGREEN GROVES

Many kinds of warblers, white-throated and Lincoln's sparrows, purple finches, flickers, hairy and downy woodpeckers, hermit thrushes, crossbills, ovenbirds, siskins, flycatchers, and others.

ON THE WATER

Ducks, teals, wild geese, rails, bitterns, yellowlegs, herons, ospreys, widgeons, loons, gulls, terns, and others. These will not come to your feeder.

This is a very general list and only a start toward many interesting hours as a bird-watcher. It's useful to know as a bird-watcher from bed that birds, like many children, often take a rest in the afternoon, so most of their feeding is done in the early morning and late afternoon.

If you were a bird, and lived on high,
You'd lean on the wind when the wind came by,
You'd say to the wind when it took you away:
"*That's* where I wanted to go today!"

When We Were Very Young

HUMMERS FOR HUMMING HUMS THROUGH

comb
tissue paper

roller, large *or* small, from
paper towels *or* tissue

The tissue paper must be long and wide enough to cover the comb.

Put the comb, covered with the tissue paper, on your lips and hum. You can hum almost any tune on your tissue-comb.

Draw and cut out some round holes for different notes on the roller, beginning about 3 inches down from the top of a long roller; 1½ inches from the top of a short roller.

Now hum tunes through the top of the roller and cover some of the notes with your fingers as you hum.

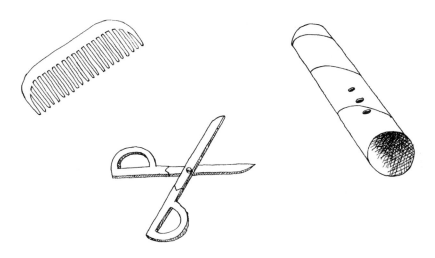

WHOSE VOICE IS IT?

Make up and practice voices for all the Pooh characters.

Do you think an Eeyore voice would sound sad and pathetic and rather whining? Also, remember he's a donkey, so he might go "hee-haw."

Piglet would certainly have a high squeaky voice.

What about Owl's? An owl goes "whoo-whoo," and sounds very serious and wise.

Kanga would probably sound like a mother; Roo would have a soft and tiny voice.

A Pooh voice would surely sound a little growly, low, and sometimes a little sticky if he was talking after he'd had a lick or two of honey.

How about Rabbit, Tigger, and Christopher Robin?

"But isn't that Rabbit's voice?"
"I don't *think* so," said Rabbit.
"It isn't *meant* to be."

Winnie-the-Pooh

TOOTHPICK OR MATCHSTICK DOODLES

Use wooden toothpicks or used-up kitchen matches.
Now begin your doodling. Here are a few ideas:

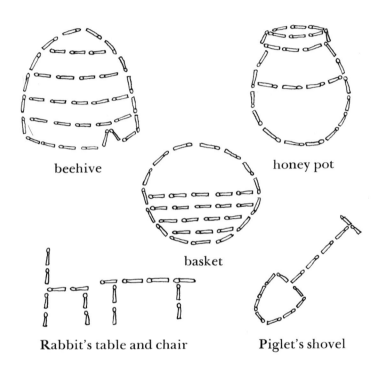

beehive

honey pot

basket

Rabbit's table and chair

Piglet's shovel

"*I* think we all ought to play Poohsticks."
So they did. And Eeyore, who had never played
it before, won more times than anybody else.

The House at Pooh Corner

TAILS AND EARS

You can make tails and ears by stuffing stockings and socks for tails and ears of different lengths and thicknesses.

If you're good at sewing, you can shape the ears by putting a few stitches along the tops to give them points, or to narrow them at the bottom. (Don't do this unless the stockings or socks are ready to be thrown out.) If you're not good at sewing, it doesn't matter: shape them with the stuffing.

Stuffing material can be scraps of paper or cloth, wool, cotton, kapok, foam rubber—any material that is soft and pliable enough to fill a rounded toe or heel of a sock or stocking.

You can then play whatever animal you've made a tail and ears for *and* practice the voice of that animal.

Pooh's ears

Eeyore's ears

Piglet's ears

Pooh's tail

Eeyore's tail

Kanga's ears and tail

Tigger's tail and ears

A lion has a tail and a very fine tail,
And so has an elephant, and so has a whale,
And so has a crocodile, and so has a quail—
They've all got tails but me.
When We Were Very Young

POOH STENCILS

heavy, pliable cardboard
scissors
tracing and tissue paper

dark pencil, crayons,
or felt-tipped pen

Draw freehand or trace outlines of Pooh characters on as heavy cardboard as you can easily cut with scissors. On pp. 74–81 of this book are pictures for tracing. First trace on tissue paper. Then use tracing paper to transfer to cardboard.

Go over the outlines with dark pencil, crayon, or felt-tipped pen.

Make a hole in the center of each outline to get a starting place for cutting.

Cut out all the cardboard inside each outline.

TO USE A STENCIL

Put the stencil down on the paper or cloth and draw along the cut edge of the stencil.

SOAP SCULPTURING IN BED

soap   newspaper
blunt-edge knife   bed table *or* tray

A large-sized cake of soap, not hard-milled, is easiest for learning how to do soap sculpture.

Draw the outline of a side view of Pooh, Piglet, Eeyore, Owl, other Pooh characters, or just heads, in pencil on the soap.

Cut triangles △ or half circles ◡ of soap from between the ears, under the arms, between the legs, or from the sides of the necks of your figure. Then cut small pieces away toward the line. As you chip and cut closer to the pencil outline, go more and more carefully.

You can make a whole set of these to put on a shelf or a bureau. Some soaps will take water colors and felt marking pencils. Wax crayons will not color soap.

One day when Pooh Bear had nothing else to do, he thought he would do something, so he went round to Piglet's house to see what Piglet was doing.

The House at Pooh Corner

POOH BOOKMARKS AND LABELS

pre-gummed labels *or*   colored pencils, crayons,
   white paper   *or* felt-tipped pens
scissors   rubber cement *or* glue, if
                            white paper is used

Measure off the white paper in squares or rectangles of a size good for a bookmark or labels for jars and honey pots, and cut them out.

Choose pictures from any of the Pooh books that you think would be good as bookmarks or to label jars or honey pots or other containers.

Draw and color them onto the pre-gummed labels or your own cut from white paper. Put your name on the bookmarks.

Stick one bookmark in each of your own books on the back cover.

Bookmarks are also good on the outside of notebooks, such as the one you may be keeping for your bird-watching.

Your mother might like a few to put on the bags or containers of foods before they're put in the freezer.

As soon as he got home, he went to the larder; and he stood on a chair, and took down a very large jar of honey from the top shelf. It had HUNNY written on it.

Winnie-the-Pooh

WALL HANGING

rollers from paper towels	crayons, paints,
paper *or* cloth	*or* felt-tipped pens
pencil	rubber cement, paste, *or* glue
stencils	ribbon *or* string
	picture hanger *or* pushpin

You can use old window shades which are clean and dry instead of rollers from paper towels and cloth or paper. If you use the rollers, this is how to make your wall hangings:

Take two rollers from used rolls of paper towels.

Measure off paper or cloth the same width as the rollers.

Make it as long as you want your wall hanging to be with enough extra to wrap around the two rollers, top and bottom.

Draw a faint pencil line on the paper or cloth *below* where it wraps around the top roller and *above* where it wraps around the bottom roller.

Use your stencils for this (see pp. 74–81) or draw freehand; then color pictures of Pooh and Tigger, Pooh and Piglet, Pooh and Eeyore, a honey pot, a beetle or two, and some flowers on the wall hanging, not in a straight line.

Use bright-colored paints, crayons, or felt-tipped pens.

When the paints are dry, put rubber cement, paste, or glue around one roller. Wrap one end of the paper or cloth around the roller so that the two stick together as smoothly as possible. Now do the other end.

Run a ribbon or string through the top roller.

Tie the ends together and pull the ribbon or string around so that the knot is inside the roller.

Your painted wall hanging should hang by the ribbon or string from a picture hanger or pushpin.

"Sometimes it's a Boat,
and sometimes it's more of an
Accident. It all depends."
Winnie-the-Pooh

A POOH PICTURE PUZZLE

On a big piece of white cardboard, draw freehand your favorite picture from *Winnie-the-Pooh* or *The House at Pooh Corner,* or use a picture from pp. 74–81 in this book.

Color it—grass, trees, sky, Pooh characters, everything. Leave very few white spaces.

Draw curvy lines *across* the cardboard picture from one side to the other:

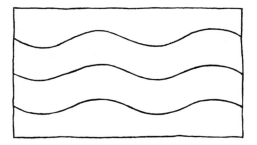

Then draw the same kind of curvy lines from top to bottom across the picture:

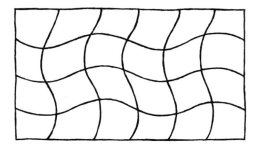

Cut along the lines and let the pieces drop into a cardboard box or small carton.

Scramble the pieces.

Now put them together again to make the picture.

For a more difficult puzzle, make the pieces of the puzzle smaller by drawing the lines across and from top to bottom over the picture closer together or in a more complicated pattern, for example:

"I thought this was *your* party."
"I thought it was *once*. But
I suppose it isn't."

Winnie-the-Pooh

POOH CHARACTERS OR FRIENDS

pads and pencils

This is a good game to play alone as well as with friends when you're allowed to have visitors.

You need a pad and pencil for each player.

First pick 3, 4, or 5 letters of the alphabet. Write them 2 inches apart at the top of your pad.

In the margin at the side, write the different categories, one under the other:

	P	L	T
Pooh Characters or Names of Friends	Piglet	Lucy	Tigger
Animals or Fish	Panther	Leopard	Trout
Birds or Reptiles	Pigeon	Lark	Turtle
Colors or Fruits	Pink	Lemon	Tan
Flowers or Vegetables	Poppy	Lilac	Turnip
Trees or Stars and Planets	Pluto	Laurel	Teak

If you fill in all the columns under all the letters, you score 500. If you do not fill in all the letters in each column, score 10 points for each one you do get.

POOH PAIRS—MATCH-A-CARD GAME
FOR 2 OR 4 PLAYERS

cardboard, white *or* colored   scissors
crayons *or* felt-tipped pens

Draw 20 rectangles with ruler on cardboard of any kind and of any color, about 3 inches long and 2 inches wide.

You will need 20 rectangles in order to have 2 each for Pooh, Piglet, Owl, Rabbit, Eeyore, Tigger, Kanga, Roo, Very Small Beetle, and Christopher Robin.

Trace or draw these 10 Pooh characters in outline in different colors. The cards are shown on pp. 69–71. Color them if you like.

Cut out the rectangles.

Shuffle the cards, so that they are well mixed.

Deal them to the players.

Hold your cards so the other players can't see what you have in your hand.

The dealer draws a card from the hand of the player to his left.

That player draws from the player on *his* left. And so on for each player.

The winner is the first player to get 3 pairs if there are 2 players, and 2 pairs if there are 4 players.

The winner calls out, "Pooh Pairs!" and puts his pairs on the table face up so the other players can count the pairs.

Rabbit

Pooh

Piglet

Owl

Roo

Tigger

Eeyore

Kanga

Alexander Beetle

Christopher Robin

"What's for breakfast?" said Pooh.
"What do *you* say, Piglet?"
"I say, I wonder what's going to happen exciting *today*?" said Piglet.
　　　　　　　　　　　　　—*Winnie-the-Pooh*

POOH AND HIS FRIENDS
FOR TRACING

Christopher Robin

Pooh and His Friends for Tracing

Pooh

 WOL

Piglet

Rabbit

Pooh and His Friends for Tracing

Kanga

Roo

A. A. MILNE was born in England in 1882, studied at Westminster School and Cambridge University, and for several years was an editor of *Punch*. In 1924 he wrote *When We Were Very Young,* a book of verse dedicated to his only son, Christopher Robin Milne. In 1926 *Winnie-the-Pooh,* which contains the first Pooh stories, was published, followed in 1927 by another book of verse, *Now We Are Six*. In 1928 more Pooh stories appeared in *The House at Pooh Corner*. Milne died in 1956.

VIRGINA H. ELLISON grew up near Poughkeepsie, New York, and was graduated from Vassar College. She lives in Stamford, Connecticut, and has two grown sons. Mrs. Ellison has been an editor and writer for a number of years. Her other Pooh-inspired books are *The Pooh Cook Book* and *The Pooh Party Book*.

ERNEST H. SHEPARD was born in 1879 and lives in Sussex, England. He illustrated all four of the Pooh books, and it is difficult to think of Pooh and his friends apart from Shepard's marvelous drawings. He also illustrated another children's classic, *The Wind in the Willows,* by Kenneth Grahame, as well as several stories of his own.

LEIGH GRANT received her art history degree from Hollins College and her fine arts degree from Pratt Institute. After studying and working in France and England, Miss Grant has returned to Greenwich, Connecticut, her hometown, to be a freelance artist. Her pen-and-ink explanatory drawings for *The Pooh Get-Well Book* add their own particular charm.